Discover South America

by Victoria Marcos

© 2014 by Victoria Mar
ISBN: 978-1-62395-638
eISBN: 978-1-62395-644-8
ePib ISBN: 978-1-62395-645-5
Images licensed from Fotolia.com
All rights reserved.
No portion of this book may be reproduced
without express permission of the publisher.
First Edition
Published in the United States by Xist
Publishing
www.xistpublishing.com
PO Box 61593 Irvine, CA 92602

South America is filled with interesting animals.

The white-faced saki lives in the lower part of the forest.

It eats mostly fruit but also eats nuts, seeds and insects.

Tamarins live in tropical rain forests. They run and jump very fast through the trees.

Most species have hair on their face that looks like a mustache.

Unlike tamarins, sloths move very slowly and only when necessary. They sleep 15-18 hours a day.

Uakari have long hair on their bodies but their heads are bald.

They can leap over 18 feet.

Howler monkeys are famous for their loud howls which can travel up to three miles through the forest.

American crocodiles are one of the largest crocodile species. They can reach up to 20 feet in length.

Geckos are small lizards that can lose their tail to get away from predators.

The emerald tree boa lives in the rain forests of South America. They are not venomous. They squeeze their prey instead of biting them.

Many chameleons have the ability to change color. Their feet have adapted to living in trees.

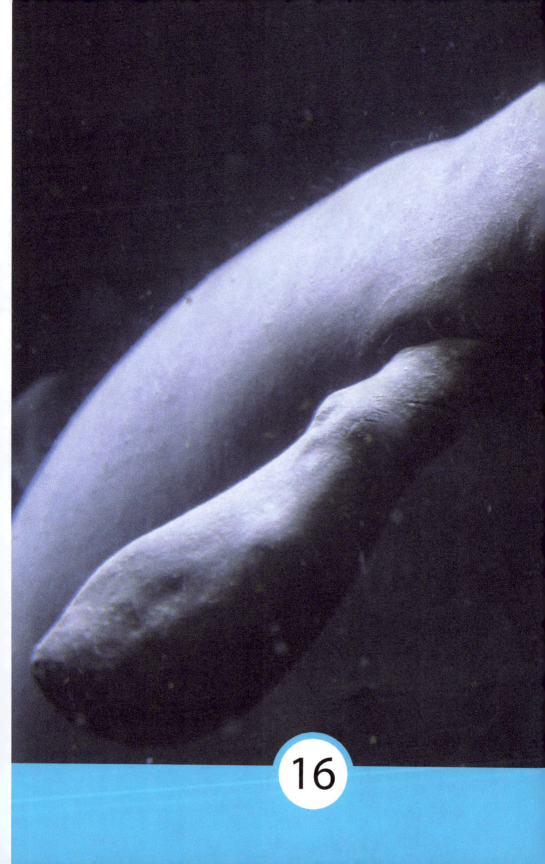

Manatees use their flippers to "walk" along the bottom of the sea floor while using their flexible upper lip to gather food.

South American tapirs are excellent swimmers. Their flexible snouts help them gather plants.

20

Tree frogs are usually tiny and spend most of their lives in trees. They are able to grasp branches very well.

This Yellow-Banded Poison Dart Frog is poisonous to the touch.

It gives a loud warning call and is very territorial.

Parrots are able to imitate, or copy, human speech. They are considered the most intelligent of all birds.

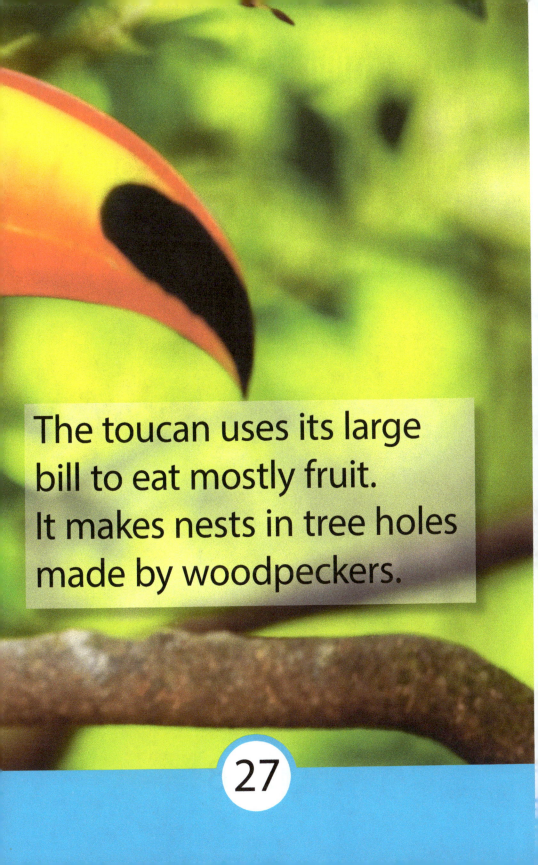

The toucan uses its large bill to eat mostly fruit. It makes nests in tree holes made by woodpeckers.

Most millipedes have between 36 and 400 legs. Since they don't bite or sting, they curl into a tight coil to protect themselves.

Stag beetles use their long jaws for fighting.
They are often found under layers of fallen wood.

Jaguars are carnivores and prefer large prey.

They are the largest cat in South America.

They can eat as much as 55 pounds of meat in one sitting.

The South American rainforest is home to many unusual animals, both large and small.

Printed in the USA
CPSIA information can be obtained
at www.ICGtesting.com
CBHW050827041224
18197CB00015B/6

9 781623 956387